States

COLORADO

by Jason Kirchner

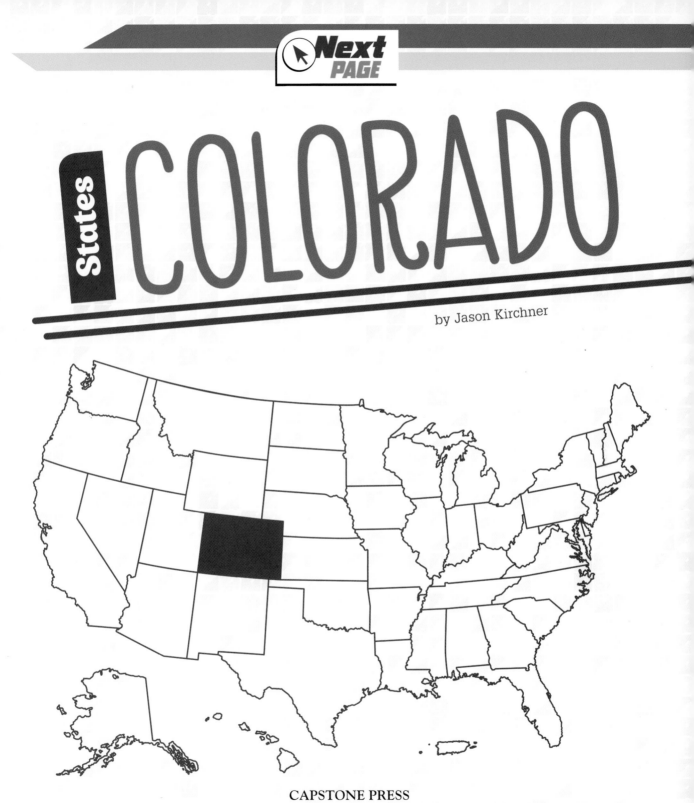

CAPSTONE PRESS
a capstone imprint

Next Page Books are published by Capstone Press,
1710 Roe Crest Drive, North Mankato, Minnesota 56003
www.mycapstone.com

Library of Congress Cataloging-in-Publication Data
Cataloging-in-publication information is on file with the Library of
Congress
ISBN 978-1-5157-0392-1 (library binding)
ISBN 978-1-5157-0452-2 (paperback)
ISBN 978-1-5157-0504-8 (ebook PDF)

Editorial Credits
Jaclyn Jaycox, editor; Kazuko Collins and Katy LaVigne, designers;
Morgan Walters, media researcher; Laura Manthe, production specialist

Photo Credits
Alamy: North Wind Picture Archives, 27; Capstone Press: Angi Gahler,
map 4, 7; CriaImages.com: Jay Robert Nash Collection, 12, top 19,
bottom left 21; Dreamstime: Mikephotos, middle 19; Getty Images:
Michael Williams/Stringer, bottom 19; Glow Images: SuperStock, 11,
middle right 21; Library of Congress: Library of Congress Prints and
Photographs Division Washington, D.C., 26; Newscom: Glasshouse
Images, bottom 18, Tim Warner/Cal Sport Media, bottom 24; One Mile
Up, Inc., 22-23; Shutterstock: Arina P Habich, 14, 16, 17, 29, BGSmith,
middle left 21, Bildagentur Zoonar GmbH, top right 21, BluIz60, top left
21, Cindy Creighton, bottom left 20, Donna Beeler, middle 18, Everett
Historical, 28, f11photo, 13, Featureflash, top 18, kan_khampanya,
cover, 5, LeicherOliver, 15, LFRabanedo, top left 20, ljh images, top
right 20, MarcelClemens, bottom right 21, Oscity, 9, robert cicchetti, 7,
SNEHIT, bottom left 8, steve estvanik, bottom right 8, treisdorfphoto,
bottom right 10, Vereshchagin Dmitry, top 24, Zack Frank, 6;
Wikimedia: Billy Hathorn, 25, Megan McCarty, bottom right 20

All design elements by Shutterstock

Printed and bound in China.
0316/CA21600187
012016   009436F16

TABLE OF CONTENTS

Want to take your research further? Ask your librarian if your school subscribes to PebbleGo Next. If so, when you see this helpful symbol (↖) throughout the book, log onto www.pebblegonext.com for bonus downloads and information.

LOCATION

Colorado is a western state. It is shaped like a box. Colorado borders several states. To the west is Utah. New Mexico lies to the south. A little piece of Oklahoma is also to the south. The southwest tip of Colorado touches Arizona. Colorado borders Wyoming to the north. Nebraska is on its northeast corner. To the east is Kansas. Denver is Colorado's capital and biggest city. Colorado's next biggest cities are Colorado Springs, Aurora, Fort Collins, and Lakewood.

PebbleGo Next Bonus!
To print and label your own map, go to www.pebblegonext.com and search keywords:
CO MAP

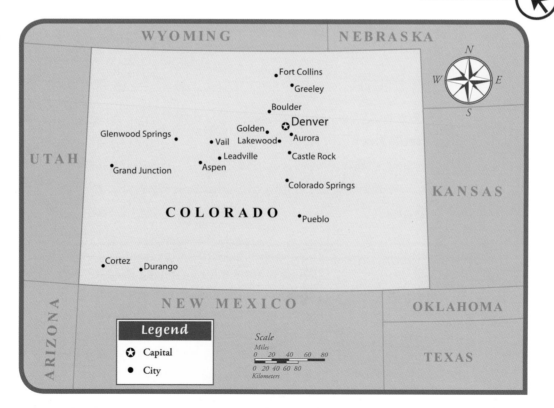

WYOMING   NEBRASKA

N
W   E
S

• Fort Collins
• Greeley
• Boulder
Golden • ☒ Denver
Glenwood Springs •   • Vail Lakewood •   • Aurora
UTAH   • Leadville   • Castle Rock
• Grand Junction   • Aspen
• Colorado Springs
KANSAS
COLORADO   • Pueblo

• Cortez   • Durango

ARIZONA   NEW MEXICO   OKLAHOMA

Legend
☒ Capital
• City

TEXAS

Scale
Miles
0 20 40 60 80
0 20 40 60 80
Kilometers

4

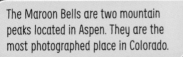

The Maroon Bells are two mountain peaks located in Aspen. They are the most photographed place in Colorado.

GEOGRAPHY

Colorado has four main land regions. They are the Rocky Mountains, the Colorado Plateau, the Intermontane Basin, and the Great Plains. The Rocky Mountains rise high over the middle of Colorado. Colorado's highest peak, Mount Elbert, is found in the Rocky Mountains. It is 14,431 feet (4,399 meters) above sea level. The Colorado Plateau is an area of high, flat land along Colorado's western border. Located in the northwest corner of Colorado, the Intermontane Basin is an area of plateaus and rolling hills. The Great Plains region in eastern Colorado is mostly flat. The area is dry and grassy.

PebbleGo Next Bonus! To watch a video about Rocky Mountain National Park, go to www.pebblegonext.com and search keywords:

CO VIDEO

The Colorado National Monument is located in the Colorado Plateau, near Grand Junction.

In addition to being the tallest peak in Colorado, Mount Elbert is also the highest mountain in the entire 3,000-mile-long Rocky Mountains.

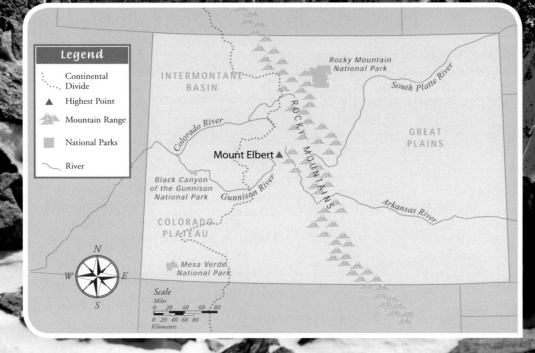

Legend

⋯⋯ Continental Divide

▲ Highest Point

🏔 Mountain Range

■ National Parks

〰 River

INTERMONTANE BASIN

Rocky Mountain National Park

South Platte River

Colorado River

ROCKY MOUNTAINS

Mount Elbert ▲

GREAT PLAINS

Black Canyon of the Gunnison National Park

Gunnison River

Arkansas River

COLORADO PLATEAU

Mesa Verde National Park

N
W E
S

Scale
Miles
0 20 40 60 80

0 20 40 60 80
Kilometers

WEATHER

Colorado is cool and dry. The average summer temperature is 65 degrees Fahrenheit (18 degrees Celsius). The average winter temperature is 25°F (-4°C).

Average High and Low Temperatures (Denver, CO)

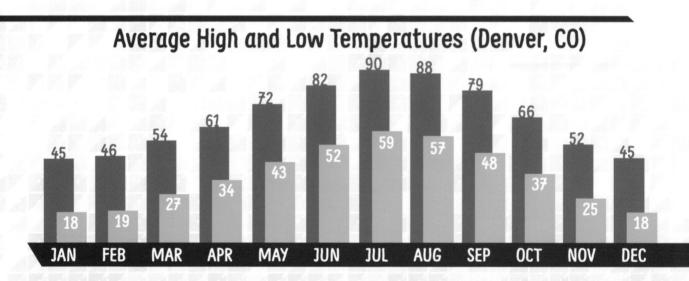

	JAN	FEB	MAR	APR	MAY	JUN	JUL	AUG	SEP	OCT	NOV	DEC
High	45	46	54	61	72	82	90	88	79	66	52	45
Low	18	19	27	34	43	52	59	57	48	37	25	18

LANDMARKS

Aspen

Aspen is a popular ski resort in the Rocky Mountains in west-central Colorado. It offers beautiful scenery for downhill skiing, snowboarding, and cross-country skiing.

Rocky Mountain National Park

Rocky Mountain National Park is in northern Colorado. The park has rugged mountain peaks, lakes, wildlife, and wildflowers. Visitors hike, fish, camp, and bike throughout much of the park's 415 square miles (1,075 square kilometers).

Buffalo Bill Museum and Grave

Buffalo Bill Museum and Grave honors scout and showman William "Buffalo Bill" Cody. On top of Lookout Mountain near Golden, the museum tells the story of Buffalo Bill's life as a U.S. Army scout, buffalo hunter, and Wild West showman.

HISTORY AND GOVERNMENT

Zebulon Pike Jr., a soldier and explorer, saw the peak now named for him while traveling in Colorado in 1806.

Hundreds of years ago, American Indians lived in Colorado. Spanish explorer Francisco Vázquez de Coronado crossed southeastern Colorado in 1541. In 1682 France claimed a large area of the present-day United States, including eastern Colorado. Then Spain claimed western Colorado in 1706. In 1803 the United States bought the eastern and central parts of Colorado from France as part of the Louisiana Purchase. Mexico won independence from Spain and claimed western Colorado in 1821. The United States took control of western Colorado after winning the Mexican War (1846–1848). In 1876 Colorado became the 38th state.

Colorado's state government has three branches. The governor leads the executive branch, which carries out laws. The legislature makes laws. It is made up of the 35-member Senate and the 65-member House of Representatives. Judges and their courts make up the judicial branch. They uphold the laws.

Colorado's state capitol building is located in Denver.

INDUSTRY

Colorado's economy is based on land types. Farming takes place on the Great Plains. Beef cattle are the leading farm product. Colorado is also a large producer of sheep. The main crops in the state are wheat, corn, and hay.

Manufacturing and service industries are located in cities along the border of the Great Plains and the Rockies. Most manufacturing jobs in Colorado are in technology. Companies in Colorado make computers and other electronic equipment, scientific instruments, and industrial robots. Many Colorado workers are in service industries. In the mountains, tourist services

Arapahoe Basin is an alpine ski area in the Rocky Mountains. It's known for its long ski seasons, lasting from October to June.

are the main business. Each year tourists spend billions of dollars at Colorado's famous skiing resorts.

Colorado's oil and coalfields lie west of the Rockies. Coal, oil, and natural gas are mined there. Molybdenum, titanium, and uranium are also mined in Colorado.

Colorado is one of the top-ranking states in the nation for sheep and wool production.

POPULATION

Coloradans come from many cultures. The gold rush brought miners from all over the world. People from central Europe came to Colorado to farm. Hispanics were the first non-Indians to settle in Colorado. Today Hispanic people make up almost 18 percent of Colorado's population. Other Coloradans have roots in Vietnam, China, and various Asian lands. Less than 3 percent of Coloradans are Asian, but they are the fastest- growing group in the state. African-Americans make up over 3 percent of Coloradans. A small number of American Indians live in Colorado. They belong to the Ute, Cheyenne, Sioux, Arapaho, and other tribes.

Population by Ethnicity

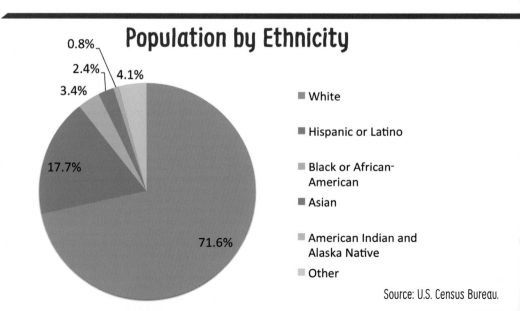

0.8%
2.4%
3.4%
4.1%
17.7%
71.6%

- White
- Hispanic or Latino
- Black or African-American
- Asian
- American Indian and Alaska Native
- Other

Source: U.S. Census Bureau.

The Denver Chalk Art Festival is held annually on Larimer Square. More than 200 artists spend a weekend filling the streets with their works of art.

FAMOUS PEOPLE

Tim Allen (1953–) is an actor and comedian. He starred in the *Santa Clause* and *Toy Story* movie series. He was born in Denver.

William F. "Buffalo Bill" Cody (1846–1917) was a U.S. Army scout and buffalo hunter who later became famous for his Wild West exhibition, Buffalo Bill's Wild West Show. He brought his show to Colorado several times and is buried on Lookout Mountain near Denver. He was born in Iowa.

Ouray (1820–1883) was a chief of the Ute Indians. He worked for peace between the Ute and white settlers. He organized the first treaty between the Ute and the U.S. government. He moved to Colorado when he was 18.

Margaret "Molly" Tobin Brown (1867–1932) was a humanitarian and socialite who survived the sinking of the *Titanic* in 1912. She was born in Missouri and later moved to Colorado. Her story was told in the musical *The Unsinkable Molly Brown*.

Scott Carpenter (1925–2013) was the second American astronaut to orbit Earth in a spacecraft. Carpenter attended the University of Colorado from 1945 to 1949. He was born in Boulder.

Ruth Handler (1916–2002) was a toy maker. She cofounded the Mattel toy company and invented the Barbie doll. She was born in Denver.

STATE SYMBOLS

Tree

Colorado blue spruce

Flower

white and lavender columbine

Bird

lark bunting

Insect

Colorado hairstreak butterfly

PebbleGo Next Bonus! For a recipe using fruit you can find in the Colorado Rockies, go to www.pebblegonext.com and search keywords:

CO RECIPE

Folk Dance

square dance

Grass

blue grama

Mammal

Rocky Mountain bighorn sheep

Fish

greenback cutthroat trout

Fossil

Stegosaurus

Mineral

rhodochrosite

FAST FACTS

STATEHOOD
1876

CAPITAL ☆
Denver

LARGEST CITY ●
Denver

SIZE
103,642 square miles (268,432 square kilometers) land area
(2010 U.S. Census Bureau)

POPULATION
5,268,367 (2013 U.S. Census estimate)

STATE NICKNAME
Centennial State

STATE MOTTO
"Nil sine Numine," which is Latin for "Nothing without
Providence"

STATE SEAL

The state seal has a picture of a shield with three snow-capped mountains and two miner's tools. A triangle at the top shows "the eye of God." The rods bound together under the triangle mean strength. The ax stands for leadership. Below the shield is the state motto, "Nil Sine Numine." It is Latin for "Nothing without Providence." At the bottom is the date 1876, the year Colorado became a state.

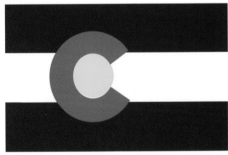

PebbleGo Next Bonus! To print and color your own flag, go to www.pebblegonext.com and search keywords: **CO FLAG**

STATE FLAG

Colorado's state flag has three horizontal stripes. The top and bottom stripes are blue. They stand for Colorado's blue skies. The middle stripe is white, for Colorado's snowy mountains. The letter "C" stands for Colorado. Inside the "C" is a gold disk. It represents the state's sunshine and its gold. The Colorado state legislature approved the flag on June 5, 1911.

MINING PRODUCTS

natural gas, petroleum, molybdenum, coal

MANUFACTURED GOODS

computer and electronic equipment, food products, chemicals, machinery, petroleum and coal products, transportation equipment

FARM PRODUCTS

beef cattle, milk, wheat, corn, hay

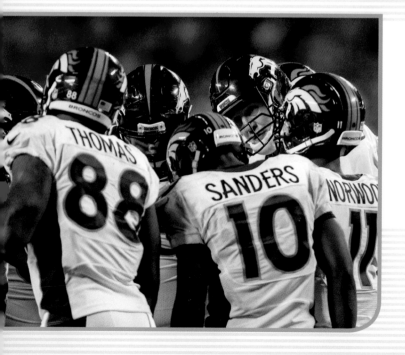

PROFESSIONAL SPORTS TEAMS

Colorado Rockies (MLB)
Colorado Rapids (MLS)
Denver Nuggets (NBA)
Denver Broncos (NFL)
Colorado Avalanche (NHL)

PebbleGo Next Bonus!
To learn the lyrics to the state song, go to www.pebblegonext.com and search keywords:

CO SONG

COLORADO TIMELINE

600–1300
Ancient Puebloans live in the cliffs of Mesa Verde in the southwest corner of Colorado.

1541
Spanish explorer Francisco Vázquez de Coronado crosses southeastern Colorado.

1620
The Pilgrims establish a colony in the New World in present-day Massachusetts.

1682
French explorer René-Robert Cavelier, known as Sieur de La Salle, claims eastern Colorado for France.

1706 Spanish official Juan de Ulibarri claims western Colorado for Spain.

1803 The United States buys a large area of land from France, including the eastern and central parts of Colorado. The sale was called the Louisiana Purchase.

1806 U.S. Army officer Zebulon Pike explores Colorado. During his travels he sees a peak in the present-day Colorado Rockies from at least 150 miles (241 kilometers) away. It is now called Pikes Peak.

1848 The United States wins the Mexican War (1846–1848) and takes control of western Colorado.

1858 Miners find gold at Dry Creek near present-day Denver. Hundreds of thousands of people travel to Colorado in the late 1850s and 1860s to look for gold.

 **1861** The U.S. Congress creates Colorado Territory.

 **1861–1865** The Union and the Confederacy fight the Civil War. Almost 4,000 men from the Colorado Territory serve in the volunteer Union forces.

1864 New settlers and American Indians fight over Colorado's land. Colonel John Chivington leads Colorado militia troops in a surprise attack on American Indians. The troops kill 200 to 400 Cheyenne and Arapaho Indians at Sand Creek near Fort Lyon in southeastern Colorado.

 **1876** Colorado becomes the 38th state on August 1.

**1893** Colorado allows women to vote. It is the second state to give women the right to vote, after Wyoming.

**1906** The U.S. Mint in Denver makes its first coins. It makes 167,371,035 gold and silver coins during its first year.

**1914–1918** World War I is fought; the United States enters the war in 1917.

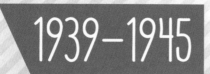**1939–1945** World War II is fought; the United States enters the war in 1941.

 **1976** Colorado celebrates its 100th birthday.

 **1995** Denver International Airport opens northeast of downtown Denver.

 **2011** Denver City Councilman Michael B. Hancock is elected mayor of Denver. He is Denver's second African-American mayor.

 **2015** Scott Jurek of Colorado sets record for fastest completion of the Appalachian Trail.

Glossary

culture *(KUHL-chuhr)*—a people's way of life, ideas, art, customs, and traditions

equipment *(i-KWIP-muhnt)*—the machines and tools needed for a job or an activity

executive *(ig-ZE-kyuh-tiv)*—the branch of government that makes sure laws are followed

exhibition *(ek-suh-BI-shuhn)*—a public display of works of art, historical objects, etc.

industry *(IN-duh-stree)*—a business which produces a product or provides a service

legislature *(LEJ-iss-lay-chur)*—a group of elected officials who have the power to make or change laws for a country or state

petroleum *(puh-TROH-lee-uhm)*—an oily liquid found below the earth's surface used to make gasoline, heating oil, and many other products

plateau *(pla-TOH)*—an area of high, flat land

region *(REE-juhn)*—a large area

rugged *(RUHG-id)*—rough and uneven, or having a jagged outline

treaty *(TREE-tee)*—an official agreement between two or more groups or countries

Read More

Altman, Linda. *Colorado.* It's My State! New York: Cavendish Square Publishing, 2014.

Ganeri, Anita. *United States of America: A Benjamin Blog and His Inquisitive Dog Guide.* Country Guides. Chicago: Heinemann Raintree, 2015.

Meinking, Mary. *What's Great About Colorado?* Our Great States. Minneapolis: Lerner Publications, 2014.

Internet Sites

FactHound offers a safe, fun way to find Internet sites related to this book. All of the sites on FactHound have been researched by our staff.

Here's all you do:

Visit *www.facthound.com*

Type in this code: 9781515703921

Check out projects, games and lots more at
www.capstonekids.com

Critical Thinking Using the Common Core

1. Colorado borders six other states. Can you name them? (Key Ideas and Details)

2. Rocky Mountain National Park is in northern Colorado. Can you name any other national parks? (Integration of Knowledge and Ideas)

3. Colorado's nickname is the Centennial State. What other nicknames do you think would be fitting for Colorado? (Integration of Knowledge and Ideas)

Index